PIANO CALM
Prayer

14 REFLECTIVE ARRANGEMENTS BY PHILLIP KEVEREN

— PIANO LEVEL —
INTERMEDIATE

ISBN 978-1-5400-9322-6

Visit Hal Leonard Online at **www.halleonard.com**

Explore the entire family of Hal Leonard products and resources

World headquarters, contact:
Hal Leonard
7777 West Bluemound Road
Milwaukee, WI 53213
Email: info@halleonard.com

In Europe, contact:
Hal Leonard Europe Limited
1 Red Place
London, W1K 6PL
Email: info@halleonardeurope.com

In Australia, contact:
Hal Leonard Australia Pty. Ltd.
4 Lentara Court
Cheltenham, Victoria, 3192 Australia
Email: info@halleonard.com.au

PREFACE

The world is a stressful place. Music can be a beautiful, calming part of tuning out the noise and recalibrating the mind, heart, and spirit. *Playing* music can be an even more effective transport into a more peaceful, restful state of mind.

Piano Calm – Prayer is a set of pieces that the intermediate pianist can enjoy as a respite from "it all." Originally arranged for a recording of the same name, I am pleased to bring it to you in sheet music form.

Sincerely,

Phillip Keveren

Piano Calm, *Piano Calm – Christmas*, and *Piano Calm – Prayer*
(Phillip Keveren, pianist) are available digitally from Burton Avenue Music
on your favorite music streaming service.

CONTENTS

ALL THINGS BRIGHT AND BEAUTIFUL

Words by CECIL FRANCES ALEXANDER
17th Century English Melody
Arranged by Martin Shaw
Adapted by Phillip Keveren

BE THOU MY VISION

Traditional Irish
Arranged by Phillip Keveren

COME, THOU FOUNT OF EVERY BLESSING

Words by ROBERT ROBINSON
Music from *The Sacred Harp*
Arranged by Phillip Keveren

With great freedom ♩ = c. 69

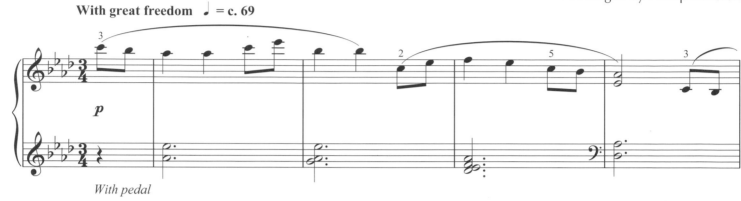

With pedal

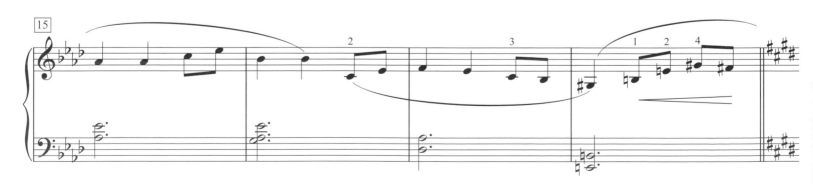

EVENING PRAYER

By PHILLIP KEVEREN

FOR THE BEAUTY OF THE EARTH

Words by FOLLIOT S. PIERPOINT
Music by CONRAD KOCHER
Arranged by Phillip Keveren

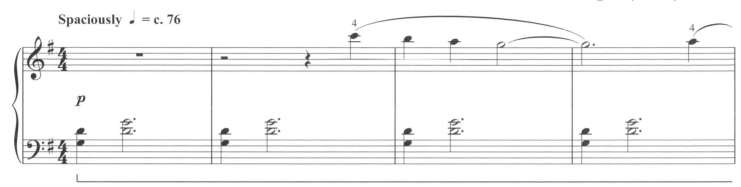

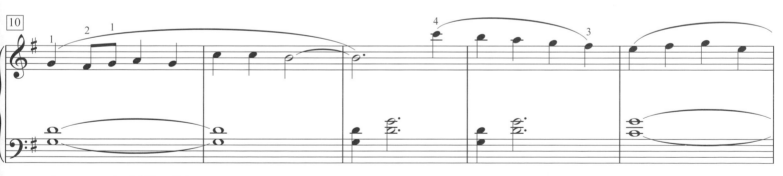

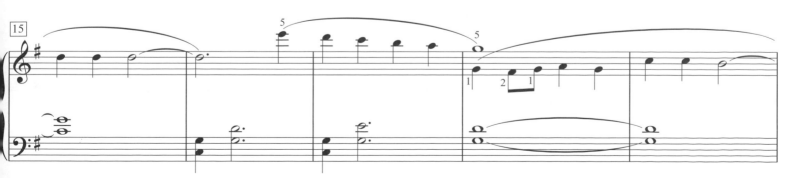

GOD LEADS US ALONG

Words and Music by G. A. YOUNG
Arranged by Phillip Keveren

HOLY, HOLY, HOLY

Text by REGINALD HEBER
Music by JOHN B. DYKES
Arranged by Phillip Keveren

Floating, with rubato ♩ = 76

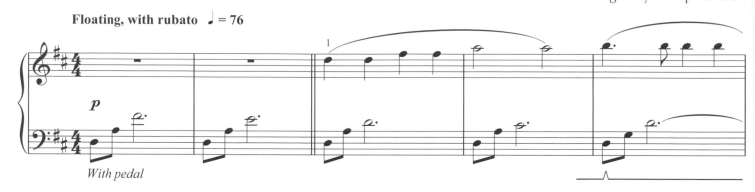

With pedal

HOW FIRM A FOUNDATION

Early American Melody
Arranged by Phillip Keveren

I'VE GOT PEACE LIKE A RIVER

Traditional
Arranged by Phillip Keveren

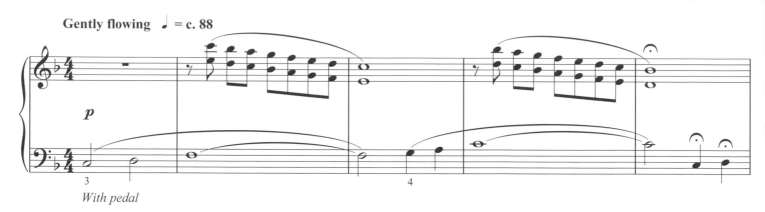

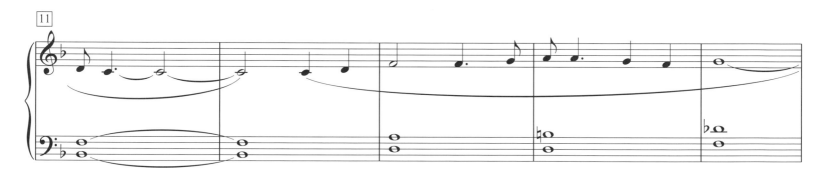

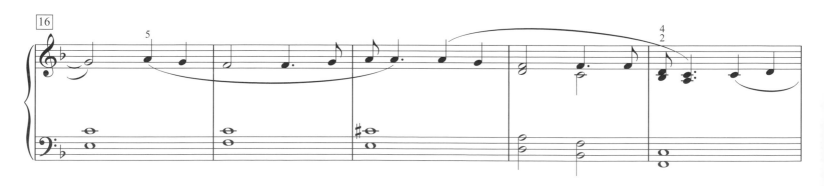

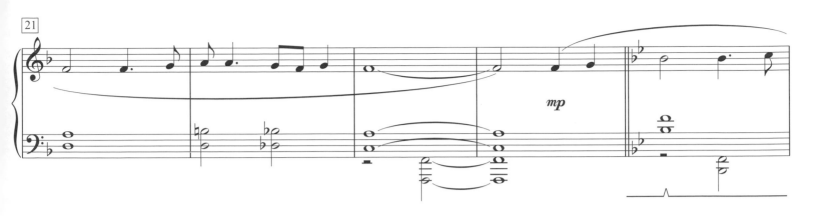

INTERLUDE

By PHILLIP KEVEREN

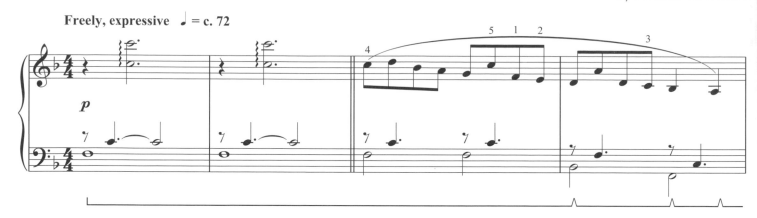

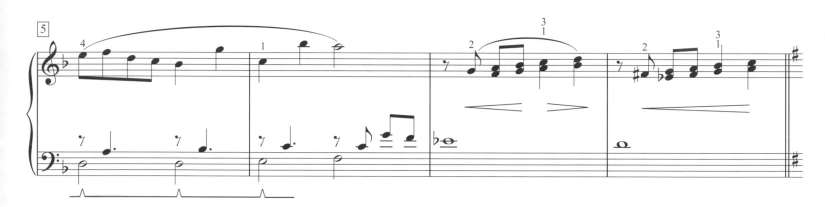

IT IS WELL WITH MY SOUL

Words by HORATIO G. SPAFFORD
Music by PHILIP P. BLISS
Arranged by Phillip Keveren

MORNING BY MORNING

By PHILLIP KEVEREN

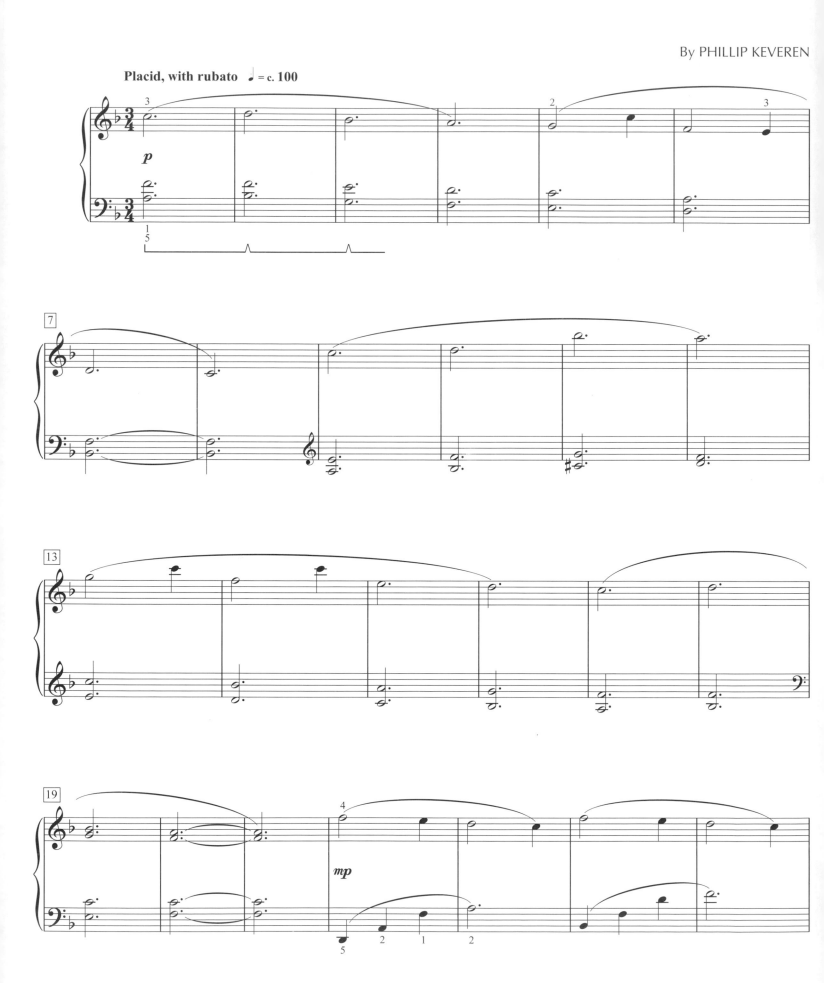

WERE YOU THERE?

Traditional Spiritual
Harmony by CHARLES WINFRED DOUGLAS
Arranged by Phillip Keveren

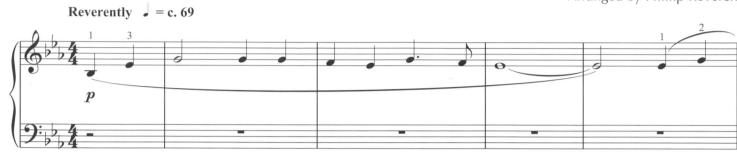

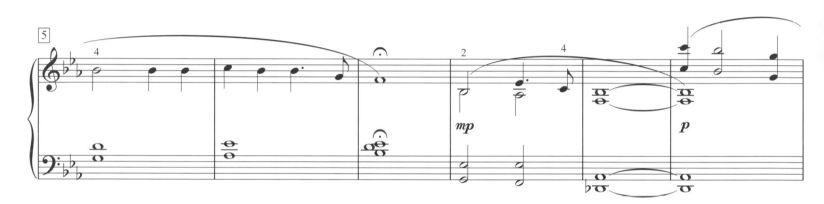

GREAT IS THY FAITHFULNESS

Words by THOMAS O. CHISHOLM
Music by WILLIAM M. RUNYAN
Arranged by Phillip Keveren

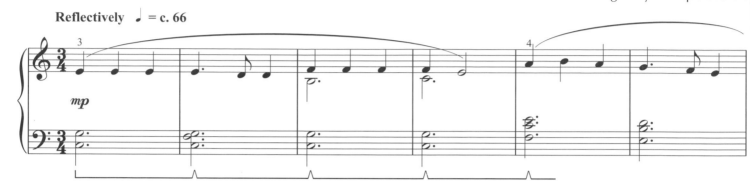

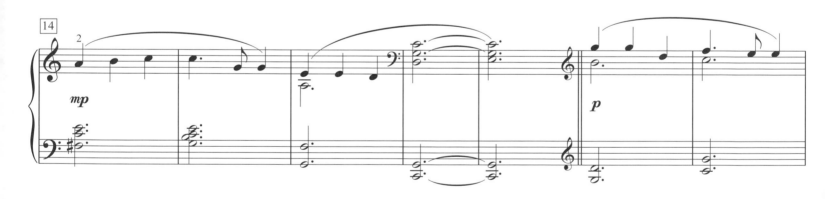

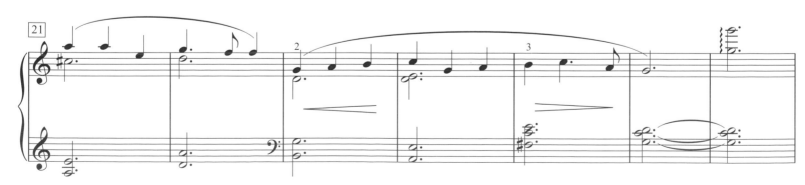

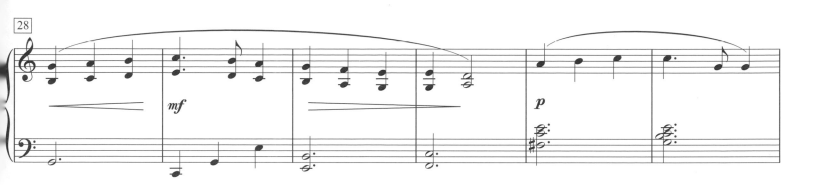

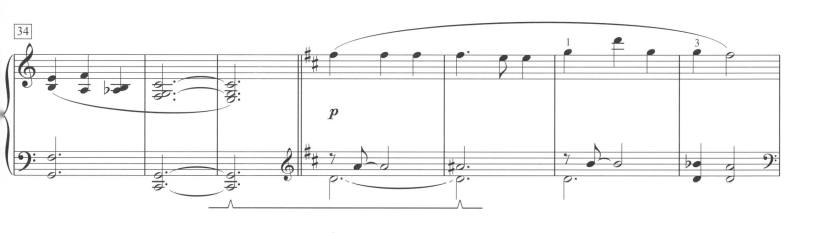

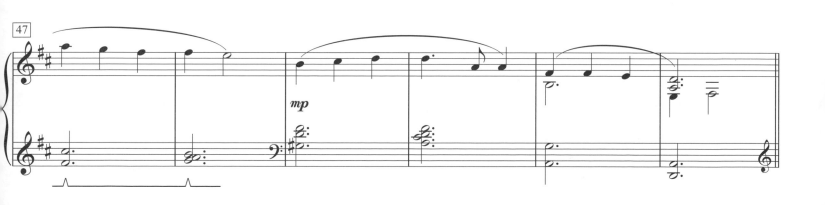

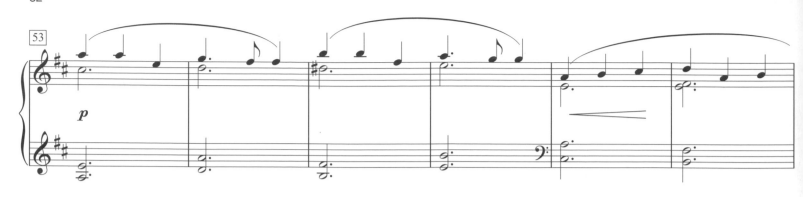

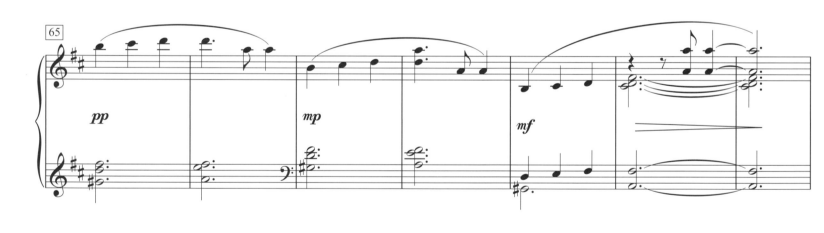

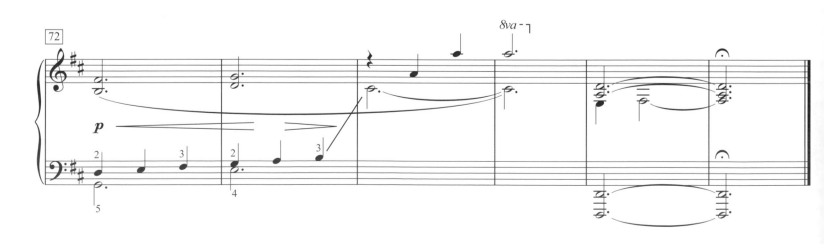